Living with Distinction:

UNDERSTANDING GOD'S PLAN FOR THE ENDTIME BELIEVER

Living with Distinction:

UNDERSTANDING GOD'S PLAN FOR THE ENDTIME BELIEVER

E.C. Nakeli

© 2017 by E.C. Nakeli
Published by King's Word Publication

For your questions and publishing needs, write to: CMFI
40 S Church St
Westminster, MD 21157
E-mail: *ecnakeli@yahoo.com*

Printed in the United States of America
All rights reserved. No part of this publication may be reproduced, stored in retrieval systems, or transmitted in any form or by any means— for example, electronic, photocopy, recording— without the prior written permission of the publisher. The only exception is brief quotations in printed reviews.
To contact the author, write to:
E.C. Nakeli
40 S Church St Westminster, MD 21157
E-mail: *ecnakeli@yahoo.com*

Living in Distinction/ E.C. Nakeli ISBN: 978-1-945055-05-8

Unless otherwise indicated, Scriptures references are from
THE HOLY BIBLE, NEW INTERNATIONAL VERSION®, NIV®
Copyright © 1973, 1978, 1984, 2011 by Biblica, Inc™
Used by permission. All rights reserved worldwide.

Table of Contents

PREFACE v

DEDICATION vi

INTRODUCTION 8
    How it used to be 10
    God's commitment 12

CHAPTER 1 15
THE DIVINE PRESENCE 15
    How to Host His Presence 25

CHAPTER 2 29
DIVINE WISDOM 29
    The distinctions of wisdom 33
    How to position yourself for wisdom 38

CHAPTER 3 45
DIVINE HEALTH 45
    What is the state of your heart? 47
    Stay Cheerful 48

CHAPTER 4 50
POWER AND AUTHORITY 50
    Three Dimensions of Power 52
    How to position yourself for power and authority ... 62

CHAPTER 5 68
VICTORY AND DOMINION 68

Your inheritance in Christ.. 69
How to align yourself for victory... 70

CHAPTER 6 76
DIVINE FAVOR 76
How to obtain favor 78
What favor does 83

CHAPTER 7 87
THE LIGHT AND GLORY OF GOD 87
Glory that exalts 90
The Canopy of Glory 90
How to activate the glory 93
Vertical and Horizontal Constraints...................... 100

CHAPTER 8 105
HOLINESS 105
Stricter Standards 107
Divine enabling 108
The Highway of Holiness 108

CHAPTER 9 111
WEALTH AND RICHES 111
Wealth without Worries 112
The Wealth of the Nations 113

PREFACE

This book, LIVING WITH DISTINCTION, is the fourth in the Christian Living series. The first book in this series is CHILD OF GOD, the second is LIVING THE ABUNDANT LIFE, and the third is LIVING A LIFE THAT COUNTS. Each book is a complete message in itself; however, together they are designed to bring believers into enjoying the fullness of the abundant life Christ Jesus brought from above. As you read, may the Holy Spirit spur in you a holy desire and passion to understand your place in the Kingdom and to enter into the fullness of life in Christ Jesus!

DEDICATION

I Dedicate this book to my beloved son Maaseiah Pele. From birth your life has been marked by distinction. When the Lord gave me the message that 2014 was going to be the beginning of living in distinction, it never crossed my mind that your miraculous birth and sustenance was going to be one of the ways the Lord would demonstrate His word. May your life and service to God be marked by distinction! May you grow up indeed as one whose Shelter is Jehovah, and you, His Wonder.

INTRODUCTION

On the early hours of December 27, 2013, at about 3:00 a.m., I suddenly got up from the bed and found that I could not fall back asleep for the next 10 minutes or so. I decided to go into the living room and pray. I prayed and worshipped the Lord in the spirit with thanksgiving. After about an hour and thirty minutes of just praise, worship and thanksgiving, the Lord dropped in my spirit that 2014 was going to be a year of distinction, opening a season during which His people will stand out distinct.

As I prayed and thanked the Lord for His word to me, a passage in Malachi 3 came to my mind. The passage is very familiar to me but as I opened and read it once again, verse 18 aroused my spirit with a quickening touch. The next day during our morning devotion, I shared the passage with my wife. I can't tell you how excited she was. I believe that we are entering a season of clear distinction as the Lord has said it so clearly in His word, "And you will again see the distinction between the righteous and the wicked, between those who serve God and those who do not" (Mal 3:18).

When you look at the Church of the Lord Jesus in this present time, it is difficult and nearly impossible, just from face value, to differentiate between true believers and false believers. The demarcation that existed in the past between the righteous and the wicked seems to have blurred out. Everybody speaks the language of the believer, sings the songs of the believer, shouts the "amen and hallelujah" of the believer. Everyone dances to the music of believers, calls the God of Israel, and quotes the Bible. Unless you are perfectly in tune with the Spirit, it is impossible to distinguish mere appearance from reality, pretense from sincerity, and the mechanisms of men from the moves of the Holy Spirit.

Does it not border you that the line that separates the church from the world and the world from the church has become blurred? Does it not grieve you that there seems to be a mass of grey instead of a clear line between black and white? The world and the church seem to have embraced each other, and the perfume of the world seems to grow stronger on the garments of the church.

How it used to be

You see, of the early church, it is written:

"The apostles performed many signs and wonders among the people. **And all the believers used to meet together in Solomon's Colonnade. No one else dared join them, even though they were highly regarded by the people.** Nevertheless, more and more men and women believed in the Lord and were added to their number. As a result, people brought the sick into the streets and laid them on beds and mats so that Peter's at least

> *Unless you are perfectly in tune with the Spirit, it is impossible to distinguish mere appearance from reality, pretense from sincerity, and the mechanisms of men from the moves of the Holy Spirit.*

shadow might fall on some of them as he passed by. Crowds gathered also from the towns around Jerusalem, bringing their sick and those tormented by impure spirits, and all of them were healed" (Acts 5:12-16, emphasis mine).

Before this time in the church, judgement had come upon Ananias and Sapphira for their falsehood. It was made clear that falsehood and hypocritical actions have no place in the house of God. God's miraculous power and holiness in the church made her distinct from the world. The people highly regarded the church because God was making His people distinct. Yet they were aware that there needs to be a distinction between them and the church and they steered clear of church gathering until they were added by the Holy Spirit.

We are about to enter another era of unprecedented and exponential demonstration of miracles, signs and wonders. People who have mocked the church will be astonished and plead to be counted as one of us because the Lord is about making a distinction.

In this present time it has also become difficult to distinguish those who are serving God for the promotion and expansion of the gospel from those who are serving their stomachs; those who are building Christ's kingdom from those who are building their personal empires; those who are investing in the kingdom and in God's people from those who are exploiting the people of God for financial gain; those who handle the things of God with care from those who treat it as an unholy thing. I sense in my spirit that the Lord is saying to the church,

"Among those who approach me I will be proved holy; in the sight of all the people I will be honored" (Lev 10:3).

God's commitment

With the proliferation of titles in the Christian church, it is difficult to distinguish between true and false servants of God. Everyone is saying "thus said the Lord", the Lord told me…" etc, but the Lord is again promising that in the sight of all people He will distinguish among His servants.

The verse we cited above (Malachi 3:18) says "You will again…" This means in the past there was a clear distinction which no longer exists, but will again exist. I am announcing to you that the time is beginning now. We are entering the season of distinction. I hear the words of the Lord to Pharaoh resounding in the air to the Pharaohs of today,

"But on that day I will deal differently with the land of Goshen, where my people live; no swarms of flies will be there, so that you will know that I, the Lord, am in this land. I will make a distinction between my people and your people" (Ex 8: 22-23a).

"But the Lord will make a distinction between the livestock of Israel and that of Egypt, so that no animal belonging to the Israelites will die" (Ex 9:4).

The families, habitations, lands, businesses, investments, property, professions, and possessions of the righteous are going to stand out from those of the masses as they did in the days of Moses.

The Lord has commissioned me to announce to you that today is the beginning of the season of distinction, and to show you how to enter into that class of those who will live in clear distinction in every area of their lives. It is a divine promise, but it is not automatic. Those who fulfill the conditions and use the right keys will enter into the realms of clear and glaring distinction.

> *The families, habitations, lands, businesses, investments, property, professions, and possessions of the righteous are going to stand out from those of the masses as they did in the days of Moses.*

It will be evident that this is the Lord's doing in your life. When you tell people you walk with the God of Israel no one will be able to doubt it because the evidences of His blessing and favor will be written all over you. When someone asks you how you are doing, you will be able to confidently and realistically say you are blessed and highly and tremendously favored and not appear ludicrous or sound ridiculous.

In this book, I am going to quickly show you the areas in which the Lord wants you to walk in distinction and how to enter into that realm of distinction. We are going to look at the factors that will make us distinct and how they will make us distinct. We are also going to look at how to position ourselves for distinction from those who are not privileged to be servants of Jehovah.

CHAPTER 1

THE DIVINE PRESENCE

One of the hallmarks of distinction between the people of God and others is the presence of the Lord. If you are to be distinct from others around you, you will have to be a carrier of the divine presence. You must have a presence-effect in the realm of the spirit and also in the physical wherever you are and in whatever you do.

If you look at those who walked in distinction in the Bible, you will notice one common factor in their lives, namely the presence of God. God promised His presence as the trump card or the guarantee for triumph and victory, wealth and riches, promotion and exaltation.

Caught in the wilderness between the place of bondage-Egypt, and the place of total freedom and establishment- Canaan, Moses made a very important plea to God saying, "How will anyone know that you are pleased with me and with your people unless you go with us? What else will distinguish me and your people from all the other people on the face of the earth?" (Ex 33:16)

The presence of God is a symbol of His pleasure with His people. That is why when the gathering of God's people is pleasing to Him, He shows up and changes lives. The presence of God will distinguish you from your surrounding as it did the

> *. If you are to be distinct from others around you, you will have to be a carrier of the divine presence. You must have a presence-effect in the realm of the spirit and also in the physical wherever you are and in whatever you do.*

Israelites from the surrounding nations.

What are the effects of the presence of God in the life of the believer? How can you host the presence of God?

1. **The Presence of God brings blessing**:

He said to Isaac,

"Stay in this land for a while,
and I will be with you and will bless you. For
to you and your descendants I will give all these lands
and will confirm the oath I swore to your father
Abraham" (Ge 26:3).

You see, the presence of God in the life of Isaac was to make him distinct in terms of the blessing that God was to pour upon him in the midst of famine. But here is the catch: Isaac had to obey the Lord and live in the midst of famine. He had to obey the Lord in spite of contrary evidences and circumstances. If you too must live in distinction you will have to walk in unconditional obedience to the divine voice. What brought the distinction to the life of Isaac is his obedience to the voice of God that came from the divine presence that was with him.

Beloved, the Lord will speak but it is our responsibility to listen and obey that voice. David said, "I will praise the Lord, who counsels me; even at night my heart instructs me" (Ps 16:7). When you carry around the presence of God, you will receive divine instructions and counsel. These will bring distinction in the area of the blessing of abundance in your life.

This promise is for you in this season of distinction, "I will instruct you and teach you in the way you should go; I will counsel you with my loving eye on you" (Ps 32:8). So position yourself in the presence of the Lord, become a carrier of the divine presence and watch the Holy Spirit instruct you in the way you should go as He did Isaac. Then you will see yourself becoming distinct.

As you fix your gaze on the Lord, you become infused with His presence and transformed into His likeness and glory. His presence in your life will make you a partaker of the eternal pleasures at His right hand.

2. **The Presence of God will fill you with joy**:

David said, "You have made known to me the path of life; you will fill me with joy in your presence, with eternal pleasures at your right hand" (Ps 16:11).

Those who host the presence of God experience joy unspeakable. In this season of distinction, as you position yourself to be a carrier of the divine presence wherever you go, watch how the Lord fills you with radiant joy. The Lord will fill your life with eternal pleasures that come from His right hand. But here is the secret to experiencing such joy unspeakable: in a previous verse, David had said, "I have set the Lord always before me…" (Ps 16: 8a).

To experience unspeakable joy, you have to set the Lord before you always, that is, your focus must be on the Lord in any, and in every situation. Refuse to take your gaze off from the Lord no matter what is happening to you. The writer of Hebrews (12:2) said you should fix your eyes on Jesus who is the author and finisher of your faith. In this way you will not grow weary or lose heart. Your life will be always full of joy.

As you fix your gaze on the Lord, you become infused with His presence and transformed into His likeness and glory. His presence in your life will make you a partaker of the eternal pleasures at His right hand. When you partake of those pleasures, greater joy becomes a part of your life.

3. **The Presence of God will bring you recognition**:

I read this in the Bible: 'This is what the Lord Almighty says: "In those days ten people from all languages and nations will take firm hold of one Jew by the hem of his robe and say, 'Let us go with you, because we have heard that God is with you'" (Ze 8:23).

As the world becomes increasingly frustrated in the system it has created and dissatisfied with life, in their desperate search for solution and for meaning, they will recognize the distinction that exists between them and servants of the Lord God. The presence of the Lord will become increasingly manifest amongst His people, and increasingly evident in their lives that the world cannot help but notice that the secret of the saints is the presence of the Lord in their midst and lives. This time, they won't be turning down our invitation to the church and gatherings of the saints, but will desperately hang on anything they can grasp to gain access into our gatherings.

> *Those who host the presence of God move ever forward to possess their inheritance in Christ Jesus. No enemy who stands on the way survives the imperial onslaught of the royal army of the eternal Majesty of the universe, because the God of victory is in our midst.*

In the previous times a hundred saints have been able to invite less than ten unbelievers to meetings, but in this season of distinction, ten unbelievers will hold on one saint to get to our meeting grounds. This also means that the spaces we now occupy won't be enough for us. A congregation of ten will become a hundred, and a congregation of a hundred shall become a thousand. We are talking of a tenfold increase that comes because of the presence of the Lord that will distinguish the gatherings of His people from other gatherings.

I am so excited. Therefore it is time to respond to this call of the Lord that says,

> "Enlarge the place of your tent,
> stretch your tent curtains wide,
> do not hold back;
> lengthen your cords,
> strengthen your stakes.
> [3] For you will spread out to the right and to the left;
> your descendants will dispossess nations
> and settle in their desolate cities" (Isa 54:2-3).

4. **The Presence of the Lord gives rest**:

The Lord told Moses, "My Presence will go with you, and I will give you rest" (Ex 33:14). There is a rest that comes to one who carries the presence of Jehovah. When the Holy Spirit is with a believer, he becomes enveloped or wrapped in the divine presence.

This brings indescribable peace to that individual even in the midst of the most uncertain of circumstances.

When the Bible talks of rest, it means that refrain from trying to make things happen in one's own capacity and ability, and trusting in the power of the Lord to work things out in one's favor. This kind of rest does not come cheap. It comes with hosting the divine presence and living in the consciousness of that presence.

When the writer of Hebrews said there is an available rest for God's people and that we should make every effort to enter that rest (see Heb 4:9-11), I believe he was referring to the rest found in hosting the divine presence.

The Lord Jesus gave an invitation to "Come to me, all you who are weary and burdened, and I will give you rest" (Matt 11:28). This means when we come to Him and stay with Him, that is, when we become hosts of the divine presence, the benefit of that hosting is the blessing of rest. In such a life there is never a cause for alarm or worry, because the divine presence brings peace and trust to he who harbors it. So, in this season of distinction, as you position yourself to host His presence, you will enter into the Sabbath rest for God's people.

5. **The Presence of the Lord brings victory and triumph**:

Those who host the divine presence walk in constant victory and triumph wherever they go. The Lord told Joshua, "Your territory will extend from the desert to Lebanon, and from the great river, the Euphrates—all the Hittite country—to the Mediterranean Sea in the west. No one will be able to stand against you all the days of your life. As I was with Moses, so I will be with you; I will never leave you nor forsake you" (Jos 1:4-5).

Those who host the presence of God move ever forward to possess their inheritance in Christ Jesus. No enemy who stands on the way survives the imperial onslaught of the royal army of the eternal Majesty of the universe, because the God of victory is in our midst.

The reason we experience so much defeat and failure is because we do not host His presence. But as we position ourselves to host His presence in this season of distinction, we will truly become the more-than-conquerors that we are. Jeremiah boldly proclaimed in the midst of violent persecution and opposition from the nation of Judah and its corrupt rulers:

> "But the Lord is with me like a mighty warrior;
> so my persecutors will stumble and not prevail.

They will fail and be thoroughly disgraced; their dishonor will never be forgotten". (Jer 20:11)

It is a very risky venture to persecute, criticize, or oppress anyone who hosts the divine presence because El Gibbor will rise up on that one's behalf. In this season of distinction we shall also behold unprecedented judgment on those who will persecute or rise up against the carriers of the divine presence. We are entering the season of dominance for those who will dare to become hosts of His victory – giving presence.

Do you remember Gideon with his three hundred men who went against the entire army of an enemy nation that oppressed the Israelites for years? The Lord told him, "I will be with you, and you will strike down all the Midianites, leaving none alive" (Judges 6:16). In this season of distinction as we become carriers of His presence, territories we shied away from in the past will become like bread to us, giants will become like ants, and mountains like molehills, because in the presence of the great Jehovah all else fades. We are possessing our possessions and extending our inheritances. Glory!

How to Host His Presence
1. Walking in humility

"For this is what the high and exalted One says— he who lives forever, whose name is holy: "I live in a high and holy place, but also with the one who is contrite and lowly in spirit, to revive the spirit of the lowly and to revive the heart of the contrite" (Isa 57:15).

In this season of distinction, the Lord will condescend to live in a manifest manner with all who will walk in complete meekness, humility, and contrition. Those whose hearts bleed for the suffering of the world, the sin of this generation, and the godlessness that seems to pervade the systems of the world will position themselves as carriers of His presence.

His presence will fill and saturate those whose hearts are broken for the current state of the church, whose hearts are broken because of the ever eroding foundations of the home and church, foundations that were laid down by the apostles and prophets. Those who respond to the hype and superficiality in the church today with contrition will become carriers of His presence.

The Psalmist said,
"The Lord is close to the brokenhearted and saves those who are crushed in spirit" (Ps 34:18). Do you want to host His presence? Mourn for His absence and walk in humility. You want to experience the closeness of the Lord, grief and groan at the immaturity that has plagued the church for generations.

2. Walking in obedience

One thing that easily causes the presence of the Lord to depart from the midst of His people is when they walk in disobedience. The Lord told Moses, "Go up to the land flowing with milk and honey. But I will not go with you, because you are a stiff-necked people and I might destroy you on the way" (Ex 33:3).

Disobedience will make the manifest presence of the Lord depart from amongst His people and from the lives of individuals. It did when Achan sinned and God withdrew from accompanying the Israelite army to battle. It did when Samson sinned and the Lord left him.

In the verse cited above, the Lord told Moses He would not accompany them into the Promised Land. He gave them the land flowing with milk and honey but withdrew from their midst because of disobedience. It is one thing to enjoy the blessings and provision of the Lord with His presence and another thing to enjoy those same blessings without His presence. The fact that you are enjoying the Lord's blessing is not a sufficient proof that the Lord is with you. In this season of distinction we must walk in total unconditional obedience to our Lord and Savior so that we position ourselves to host His presence.

3. Praying in the Spirit

The presence of Jehovah comes amongst His people in the Person of the Holy Spirit. When you pray in the Holy Spirit, you activate the presence of the Lord around you and set yourself on flames in the realm of the spirit, flames that signify the presence of Jehovah as it did when He appeared to Moses in the burning bush.

When you pray in the Holy Spirit, there is an outflow of the divine presence in you to saturate you externally. Praying often in the Holy Spirit makes you a partaker of the Lord Jesus Christ's ministry of intercession. As you share in His burden for the world through intercession His presence will increasingly saturate you and become evident to your surroundings.

4. Walking in righteousness and holiness

Nothing hinders the presence of the Lord like sin. If you are to host God's presence, you must rid yourself of all known sin and anything in your life which doesn't please the heart of the Lord. As you endeavor to walk in holiness and righteousness, the divine presence will be made manifest in your life and make you distinct from those around you.

> *His presence will fill and saturate those whose hearts are broken for the current state of the church, whose hearts are broken because of the ever eroding foundations of the home and church, foundations that were laid down by the apostles and prophets. Those who respond to the hype and superficiality in the church today with contrition will become carriers of His presence.*

CHAPTER 2
DIVINE WISDOM

One of the virtues that distinguish between people is the wisdom they have. In this season of distinction, the righteous will walk in uncommon wisdom that will baffle the heathen. The Bible says wisdom is the principal thing in life; therefore he who distinguishes himself in the domain of wisdom will be distinguished in every other domain in life.

Some of the Jewish exiles in Babylon distinguished themselves by proving ten times better than all their competitors Even as foreigners, they beat the Babylonians in their literature, history, science and every other related matter. In this season of distinction those who position themselves to walk in wisdom will beat their competitors hands down in their own very domain. It is written, "In every matter of wisdom and understanding about which the king questioned them, he found them ten times better than all the magicians and enchanters in his whole kingdom" (Dan 1:20).

We are entering the season of "ten times better" wisdom. In business we shall be ten times better. In the arts, sciences, and technology we shall distinguish ourselves by the wisdom that the Lord is imparting on those who serve Him and walk according to His ways. Because we are entering the season of distinction marked by uncommon wisdom, failure and loss are things of the past.

Wisdom is a gift from God, and He has determined to pour out that wisdom to His own to make them distinct from those who possess the wisdom of the world. Remember the young man called Stephen in the Bible. It is written, "Opposition arose, however, from members of the Synagogue of the Freedmen (as it was called)—Jews of Cyrene and Alexandria as well as the provinces of Cilicia and Asia—who began to argue with Stephen. But they could not stand up against the wisdom the Spirit gave him as he spoke" (Acts 6:9-10).

It was Stephen against a multinational, multiregional, and multi-provincial committee of Jews engaged in the heated argument about the gospel. God so filled Stephen with wisdom that his adversaries were no match to him. Take note of the description the Bible gives here? It says they could not stand up against the Spirit-inspired wisdom of Stephen. They were so disgraced that they resorted to killing him. Get ready to demonstrate wisdom that will leave your

> We are entering the season of "ten times better" wisdom. In business we shall be ten times better. In the arts, sciences, and technology we shall distinguish ourselves by the wisdom that the Lord is imparting on those who serve Him and walk according to His ways.

opponents and competitors open mouthed.

This wisdom is not going to be in any way limited. We will take the wisdom to different areas of society and replace that worldly wisdom which has proven ineffective in solving the problems of this world. Do you remember Daniel? The Bible says of him, "Now Daniel so distinguished himself among the administrators and the satraps by his exceptional qualities that the king planned to set him over the whole kingdom" (Dan 6:3).

Godly wisdom is the answer to the dilemmas that have caught the world between a rock and a hard place. It is the answer to the failed leadership we see all around us. In this season of distinction, God is placing His agents of change and better leadership at the helm of the pillars of society using the weapon of wisdom. Get ready to be recognized as a distinguished brother or sister.

We are talking here of life-saving wisdom like the one Joseph demonstrated when he interpreted pharaoh's dreams. This wisdom we are talking of will take us into the realm of nations-preserving policies. Men will invite us to enact policies that will turn economies and institutions around for the better. Are you not tired of the numerous failed policies enacted by the heathen?

Such policies generated by worldly wisdom can only sustain things temporarily before they deteriorate at a rate faster than gravity on Jupiter. The policies enacted by Joseph preserved Egypt and the surrounding nations from the destructive effect of seven years of severe famine, and turned Egypt into a regional superpower at the time. This is the kind of world-changing, kingdom building wisdom- that will come upon the righteous in this season of distinction.

It will be inappropriate to talk about wisdom yet ignore the wisest human being who has ever lived after the fall of man. This man Solomon was so wise that he became a royal celebrity among royals of the world. Kings and queens went on pilgrimage just to interact with King Solomon. Men and women of all lands sought to listen to him. It became a life time accomplishment to have an audience with King Solomon because of the wisdom with which he spoke. In this season of distinction, God will so fill His people with the spirit of wisdom that the world around you will seek audience with you, and consider it a rare privilege to hear you speak. Get ready for divine wisdom.

> *God is placing His agents of change and better leadership at the helm of the pillars of society using the weapon of wisdom. Get ready to be recognized as a distinguished brother or sister.*

The distinctions of wisdom

How then will wisdom make you distinct? We have already discussed a couple (amongst hundreds) of them in the foregoing section, but will recapitulate and highlight just a couple of them.

1. Wisdom will bring you into the service of the great

Daniel's wisdom brought him into the service of the king of Babylon and gave him government supervisory powers over other administrators in the kingdom. He was not only an administrator; he was the administrator of administrators.

Daniel was like the prime minister, the minister of ministers. He did not only serve in one government but in at least three consecutive royal administrations. Do you see that? When godly wisdom is evident in your life men will seek your service. Like Daniel, God so filled Joseph with wisdom that Pharaoh showed him goodwill and promoted him. This brings us to the next point.

2. Wisdom brings uncommon promotion

If Joseph left the prison to the palace it was because of his God-endowed wisdom that was noticed by royalty. His wisdom brought a supernatural solution to a crisis that could have paralyzed the whole Middle Eastern region and brought civilization to its knees. We are talking about the promotion that takes one from prisoner to prime minister.

3. Wisdom will bring you honor

What made other royalties honor Solomon was the wisdom with which he was blessed. His wisdom so distinguished his kingdom from other kingdoms that Israel became a center of tourism. People brought diverse gifts to honor Solomon with. In this season of distinction I see you being honored because of the divine wisdom that is coming into you. Men who have despised you until now will celebrate you because of the wisdom God will endow you with as you rightly position yourself.

4. Wisdom will protect you

One of the chief blessings of wisdom is its capacity to keep one protected and in safety. Those who possess wisdom are spared from the mistakes and follies of those who lack it. Several verses in Proverbs and Ecclesiastes in the Bible talk about the safety and protection that wisdom provides. Wisdom and prudence walk closely together so, if you possess wisdom you will also be very prudent and therefore avoid loss and injury.

5. Wisdom will extend your life

Those who walk in divine wisdom extend their days here on this earth. Wisdom will give you extra time to enjoy the blessing Jehovah gives you on this side of eternity. The Bible says through wisdom your days will be many, and then as if that was not enough, years also will be added to your life. In this season of distinction, the righteous will no longer be concerned with premature death because the wisdom the Lord will give them with will make their days many and extend their years on this planet. I believe we will be having a new problem; believers will begin to live so long that they will accomplish their purpose and still have extra time to spare. Many will start desiring to go home instead of staying, "For through wisdom your days will be many, and years will be added to your life" (Pr 9:11).

6. Wisdom will bring you creative excellence

Creative excellence is one of those factors that distinguish people on this earth. In this season of distinction, God is releasing creative excellence upon his people who have a heart for kingdom expansion and service of God's people. For the church in the wilderness, God filled some people with creative excellence so that they could build His tabernacle and design garments of splendor for the priests.

I believe we have come to the place of a repeat of such display of creative excellence amongst the people of God. We will witness the raising up of Bezaliels and Oholiabs in this season. The world thinks it has seen designers, but watch as God begins to raise designers in the kingdom whose talent will make those of the world seem like amateurs. It is written:

> "[30] Then Moses said to the Israelites, "See, the Lord has chosen Bezalel son of Uri, the son of Hur, of the tribe of Judah, [31] and he has filled him with the Spirit of God, with wisdom, with understanding, with knowledge and with all kinds of skills— [32] to make artistic designs for work in gold, silver and bronze, [33] to cut and set stones, to work in wood and to engage in all kinds of artistic crafts. [34] And he has given both

him and Oholiab son of Ahisamak, of the tribe of Dan, the ability to teach others. ³⁵ He has filled them with skill to do all kinds of work as engravers, designers, embroiderers in blue, purple and scarlet yarn and fine linen, and weavers—all of them skilled workers and designers" (Ex 35:30-35).

> I believe we have come to the place of a repeat of such display of creative excellence amongst the people of God. We will witness the raising up of Bezaliels and Oholiabs in this season. The world thinks it has seen designers, but watch as God begins to raise designers in the kingdom whose talent will make those of the world seem like amateurs

How to position yourself for wisdom
1. The fear of the Lord
"The fear of the Lord is the beginning of wisdom; all who follow his precepts have good understanding. To him belongs eternal praise" (Ps 111:10).

To fear the Lord is to walk according to His precepts. When you direct your life in accordance with the word of God you operate at a level of wisdom that others who live in neglect for the word will never do. There is a lot of wisdom in the word for those who are open to the illuminating power of the Holy Spirit. You can never act foolishly when you live in accordance with the word of God made alive in your spirit by the Holy Spirit. Let the fear of the Lord fill your life and wisdom will be your companion.

2. Ask for wisdom

One way to position yourself for the wisdom that is coming upon the saints in this season of distinction is to ask God for wisdom. Wisdom comes from God and if you must receive you must ask. In James 1:5, the Bible says, "If any of you lacks wisdom, you should ask God, who gives generously to all without finding fault, and it will be given to you." Ask for wisdom, ask in faith and ask desperately. An example of someone who asked and received is Solomon. The wisdom he received from asking distinguished him from all others who ever existed before or after him. This is what the Bible has to say about the wisdom that God gave Solomon:

> "[29] God gave Solomon wisdom and very great insight, and a breadth of understanding as measureless as the sand on the seashore. [30] Solomon's wisdom was greater than the wisdom of all the people of the East, and greater

than all the wisdom of Egypt. ³¹ He was wiser than anyone else, including Ethan the Ezrahite—wiser than Heman, Kalkol and Darda, the sons of Mahol. And his fame spread to all the surrounding nations. ³² He spoke three thousand proverbs and his songs numbered a thousand and five. ³³ He spoke about plant life, from the cedar of Lebanon to the hyssop that grows out of walls. He also spoke about animals and birds, reptiles and fish. ³⁴ From all nations people came to listen to Solomon's wisdom, sent by all the kings of the world, who had heard of his wisdom" (1Kgs 4:29-30).

God is raising people in the caliber of Solomon in terms of the wisdom they will display in this season of distinction.

3. Seek wisdom

There is a level beyond asking where we get to seeking for wisdom. Wisdom is in levels and seeking wisdom gives you access into an entirely new dimension that those who stay at the level of asking do not access. Wisdom personified says, "I love those who love me, and those who seek me find me...Blessed are those who listen to me, watching daily at my doors, waiting at my doorway. For those who find me find life and receive favor from the Lord" (Pr 8:17, 34-35).

Nothing priceless comes cheap. If you want wisdom that distinguishes you from your surrounding you've got to seek for it. The verses cited above are spoken in first person because wisdom in the person of the Lord Jesus Christ is speaking. So pursue the Lord, seek Him with your whole heart and when you find Him, there will be a transfer of divine wisdom into you, wisdom that will marvel your contemporaries.

4. Grow in Christlikeness

The Bible says Christ Jesus has become for us our wisdom from God (see 1Co 1:30). This means that the more of Christ you put on, the wiser you become. As you allow the life of Christ to fill you, His wisdom will also increasingly fill you. Make it your goal to grow in Christlikeness and you will grow in wisdom. Those who distinguish themselves in the domain of Christlikeness will become distinct in the wisdom they exercise.

5. Fill your mind with the word of God

God's word is the primary source of wisdom the Father has given us. Those who read, meditate and act on the word of God become filled with God's own wisdom. As you fill your life with the word of God you are filling your life with God's own wisdom. Saturate your life with the word of God and watch yourself walk in unprecedented wisdom. Throughout the book of proverbs you find the Lord talking of His word as a source of wisdom. Embrace the word and embrace wisdom. Walk according to the word and walk according to wisdom.

6. Ask for the Spirit of wisdom

There is another level of possessing wisdom that is beyond just having the gift of wisdom. This is the domain of the spirit of wisdom. It is one of the seven spirits of God that rested upon the Lord Jesus Christ when He walked the earth (Isa 11:2). Those who possess the Spirit of wisdom operate in supernatural wisdom as our glorious Lord did. The apostle Paul prayed that the believers will walk in similar wisdom when he wrote, "I keep asking that the God of our Lord Jesus Christ, the glorious Father, may give you the Spirit of wisdom and revelation, so that you may know him better" (Eph 1:17). It is the Spirit of wisdom that makes the difference in revelation and knowledge of God. So if you want to walk in greater wisdom, do not just ask for wisdom, ask for the Spirit of wisdom.

7. Seek for impartation

There is a short cut to uncommon wisdom, the Spirit of wisdom. Just as God has ordained that things of the Spirit be transferable through impartation, it is possible for the Spirit of wisdom to be transferred to an individual through impartation. The only limitation here is that you can only receive to the extent possessed and released by the person carrying out the impartation. If you want unlimited measure of wisdom then you have to pay the price to receive directly from the Lord. However, since many may not be in the position of persistently seeking the Lord for the Spirit of wisdom, those who really want to walk in wisdom can receive an impartation of the Spirit of wisdom from those who are filled with him. This was the situation of Joshua.

The Bible says, "Now Joshua son of Nun was filled with the spirit of wisdom because Moses had laid his hands on him. So the Israelites listened to him and did what the Lord had commanded Moses" (De 34: 9).

Moses imparted Joshua with the spirit of wisdom and he became a voice that people listened to and obeyed. In this season of distinction, wisdom will make you a voice to your generation. Men and women will hear you and obey you because they will recognize the spirit of wisdom operating in your life. Those who have heretofore ignored you will seek your counsel and obey your command because of the impartation of wisdom. Seek someone operating with the spirit of wisdom and have him impart to you the same spirit.

8. Seek by association

Here is an easy way to position yourself for wisdom, "Walk with the wise and become wise..." (Pr 13:20a). If you want to grow in wisdom, keep company with those who have a track record of wisdom. Wisdom is one of those virtues which can rub over if you stay in close proximity to those who possess divine wisdom. In this season of distinction, the Lord will bring you in contact with men and women especially endowed with wisdom. If there is no other way, get wisdom by association!

> *In this season of distinction, wisdom will make you a voice to your generation. Men and women will hear you and obey you because they will recognize the spirit of wisdom operating in your life.*

CHAPTER 3
DIVINE HEALTH

One of the areas where God has always intended for his people to walk in distinction from the rest of the world is in the area of health. The Lord wants us to walk in divine health and so He bore all of our sicknesses, diseases, and infirmities on the cross of Calvary. It is written, "He took up our infirmities and bore our diseases" (Matt 8:17) and that "He himself bore our sins" in his body on the cross, so that we might die to sins and live for righteousness; "by his wounds you have been healed" (1 Pe 2:24).

If we want to be honest with ourselves, we will acknowledge the fact that just a privileged few have entered into this inheritance of divine health. We see the same diseases, sicknesses, infirmities that afflict the unrighteous manifesting in the midst of God's own people at a deplorable rate. In this season of distinction the saints are going to arise and enter their inheritance of divine health, not just a few but multitudes will position themselves to enter their inheritance in Christ.

There is a group of people in the scriptures who distinguished themselves from their contemporaries by looking healthier in every way it could be described. The Bible says about Daniel and his friends that, "At the end of the ten days they looked healthier and better nourished than any of the young men who ate the royal food" (Da 1:15).

This is the kind of distinction in health that we the saints are entering. The diseases that afflict the unrighteous will have no place in the bodies of the righteous, because like Daniel and his friends, we are keeping away from all defilement. One of the benefits of the distinction that will come because of the abiding presence of Jehovah in the midst of His people will be healthy well-nourished bodies. This has always been the divine will for God's people as we see even in the case of the church in the wilderness.

When the Lord brought the children of Israel up out of Egypt 'He said, "If you listen carefully to the Lord your God and do what is right in his eyes, if you pay attention to his commands and keep all his decrees, I will not bring on you any of the diseases I brought on the Egyptians, for I am the Lord, who heals you" (Ex 15:26). So what we are saying about distinction in health is not quite new. The Lord willed it then and wills it now for those who are called by His Name.

As we obey His commands to not be anxious for anything, not be bitter against anybody, not harbor any form of anger, malice, or hatred in our hearts towards whomever, the diseases of the unrighteousness will not near our tents. As you saturate your life with the word of God and live it out, your soul will prosper and therefore your health also will prosper. You are only as healthy as your soul is healthy, that is, your health rotates around your emotions, your will, and your mind (see 3Jn :2). Develop healthy emotions, healthy thoughts, and a determined will and see whether you will not walk in divine health.

What is the state of your heart?
"A heart at peace gives life to the body, but envy rots the bones" (Pr 14:30).

Your heart has to be at rest and at peace if you must walk in divine health. Be at peace with yourself and with the people around you. Many of the sicknesses and diseases that afflict the people of God are as a result of hearts that are at war with themselves and with others. When there is sin in your heart, it will lead to guilt and therefore to a civil war within you and deprive your body of necessary vitality. There are many people who are mobile civil wars. No place where there is civil war ever remains the same. Destruction of vital resources and life-giving necessities lead to deterioration in health.

For some people, their problem is not that they are at war with themselves; their problem is they are always fighting with others. Their thoughts and attitude are always in a war mode with the people around them. They want to be like everybody else and possess everything that everybody else has and occupy everybody else's position. And because they are not able to achieve this, it results in envy. Envy in the heart rots the bones. Purge your heart of every form of envy and see yourself walk in divine health and be distinct from the world in this season of distinction.

> *Discouragement, self-pity, and depression are champions at crushing the human defense mechanism.*

Stay Cheerful
"A cheerful heart is good medicine, but a crushed spirit dries up the bones" (Pr 17:22).

A sad or serious look is not a mark of spirituality, it only leads to physical unfitness. Everything that is associated with low morals has a potential to crush the human spirit and give way to sickness and disease. Discouragement, self-pity, and depression are champions at crushing the human defense mechanism. That is why throughout scripture the Lord told His servants to not be discouraged. When Elijah got into a depressive state and desired death, the Lord concurred and asked him to get ready to go home.

Cheerfulness and joy in the Holy Spirit will give life to your bones and make you live healthy. Refuse to allow anything to steal away your joy and destroy your divine health. Remember we said before that in this season of distinction, there will be an anointing of joy from the Lord as we carry His

> *As we obey His commands to not be anxious for anything, not be bitter against anybody, not harbor any form of anger, malice, or hatred in our hearts towards whomever, the diseases of the unrighteousness will not near our tents.*

presence with us. This anointing of joy will act as preventive medicine from sickness and disease.

CHAPTER 4

POWER AND AUTHORITY

One thing that distinguished our Lord Jesus from the religious leaders in the days of His earthly ministry was the power and authority with which He spoke and taught the word. People are able to distinguish words spoken with power and authority from mere shouting or religious noise making. Just as in the days of Jesus the Christ, those who must distinguish themselves in these days of "please me gospel" or "the law gospel" must be those who walk in the power and authority of the cross made possible by the anointing of the Holy Ghost.

People were amazed at the Lord Jesus because He walked in power and authority. Look at the following verses:

"When Jesus had finished saying these things, the crowds were amazed at his teaching, ²⁹ because he taught as one who had authority, and not as their teachers of the law" (Mt 7:28-29).

"The people were amazed at his teaching, because he taught them as one who had authority, not as the teachers of the law" (Mk 1:22).

> *People are able to distinguish words spoken with power and authority from mere shouting or religious noise making.*

There is a difference between empty words and words which come with power and authority. People know it when you speak words that are empty even if you speak at the top of your voice. That is why the people who listened to Jesus were able to sense the authority that accompanied His words. The people were able to distinguish Him from the teachers of the law just by the authority of His words.

Ladies and gentlemen, to walk in distinction, seen and unseen people must sense the authority that accompanies the words you speak. Things and people respond to authority, and authority brings distinction.

The authority that the Lord Jesus demonstrated did not end in words only but extended to the demonstration of power. It is written that "All the people were amazed and said to each other, "What words these are! With authority and power he gives orders to impure spirits and they come out!" (Lk 4:36).

Three Dimensions of Power

The kingdom of God is the kingdom of power. The apostle Paul stated categorically that, "But I will come to you very soon, if the Lord is willing, and then I will find out not only how these arrogant people are talking, but what power they have. [20] For the kingdom of God is not a matter of talk but of power" (1Co 4:19-20).

I will repeat: these days of distinction, God is going to make His servants stand out by the power they demonstrate as they serve in the kingdom. We have heard a lot of noise going around, a lot of titles before the names of men. After you have spoken, men will want to see what comes next.

Just as Paul was going to find out what power those talkers had, so in these days of distinction the powers that be will find out what power those who claim to be serving the Lord have. Earlier Paul had stated that "My message and my preaching were not with wise and persuasive words, but with a demonstration of the Spirit's power" (1Co 2:4). Everyone bearing witness to the Lord must be ready to be used by the Lord in demonstrating power. What power do you have?

The first dimension of power

Since the kingdom of God is a kingdom of power, no one can become part of it without power. It takes power to be a part of the kingdom and to live the kingdom life. It takes power to forcefully lay hold of the kingdom and advance with it. Remember that "…from the days of John the Baptist until now, the kingdom of the heavens is taken by violence, and [the] violent seize on it" (Mt 11:12, Darby).

> *In these days of distinction, God is going to make His servants stand out by the power they demonstrate as they serve in the kingdom. We have heard a lot of noise going around, a lot of titles before the names of men. After you have spoken, men will want to see what comes next.*

For us to advance forcefully, the Lord begins by giving us power to become children of God. Without this power we are neither able to become God's children nor to live the Christian life. It is written, "But as many as received him, to them gave he power to become the sons of God, even to them that believe on his name" (Jn 1:12, KJV).

This is the power to begin the Christian life and live it. Sad to say it is the only dimension of power that many people know. They begin their Christian life with this power and depart from the scene having only experienced this level of power. This is the power that makes you overcome sin and live above the influences of the flesh and the devil. It is the power that makes you endure persecution from the world and still stand for the Lord. It is the same power the seventy-two used to defeat the enemy when Jesus sent them out in pairs to proclaim the kingdom of God.

He told them, "Behold, I give unto you power to tread on serpents and scorpions, and over all the power of the enemy: and nothing shall by any means hurt you" (Lk 10:19, KJV). The disciples were still operating in this first dimension of power when Jesus said this, because at this time they were not yet baptized in the Holy Spirit since Jesus had not yet been glorified. In these last days men and women will be awaken to consciousness of the power that they have in them simply by choosing to receive Jesus and to believe in His Name. So every child of God is supposed to be a *"trampler"* of snakes and scorpions and over all the powers of the enemy.

The second dimension of power

The second dimension of power is for those who have exercised the full extent of the first dimension and proven faithful to use it constructively for the Kingdom. It is what the Bible calls the power of the Holy Spirit. When Jesus was leaving His disciples, He told them, "But ye shall receive power, after that the Holy Ghost is come upon you: and ye shall be witnesses unto me both in Jerusalem, and in all Judaea, and in Samaria, and unto the uttermost part of the earth" (Acts 1:8).

The first dimension of power is power to become a child of God and live as one. That is its primary purpose. Although the disciples used this dimension of power to cast out demons and heal the sick when Jesus sent them out, it cannot be as effective as the second dimension of power, which is the power to testify of Jesus's death and resurrection. The unique purpose of this second dimension of power is to be God's effective witness through the testimony of Jesus Christ; His death and resurrection.

Those who refuse to embrace the baptism of the Holy Ghost with evidence of speaking in tongues forfeit their right to this dimension of power. Only the coming upon by the Holy Spirit and being filled by the Holy Spirit initiates one into this dimension of power to be an effective witness for the Lord. This dimension of power opens doors for the operation of the gifts of the Holy Spirit in the lives of those who have been baptized into the Holy Spirit with evidence of speaking in new tongues.

According to Peter, baptism into the Holy Spirit is a fulfillment of the prophecy of Joel as we will see later. In these days of distinction the Lord is releasing to His church power like never before. It is power and authority that will draw the line between the world and the church of Jesus Christ. Power to heal the sick, cast out demons, raise the dead, and set free captives will become part and parcel of the ministries of those who take their rightful place as carriers of the divine presence in these days of distinction. However, power and authority do not come like that; they are products of the anointing. Jesus was able to teach with authority and perform miracles with power because at some point He had declared that:

"[18]The Spirit of the Lord is on me,
because he has anointed me
to proclaim good news to the poor.
He has sent me to proclaim freedom for the prisoners
and recovery of sight for the blind,
to set the oppressed free,
[19] to proclaim the year of the Lord's favor" (Lk 4:18-19).

It is the anointing of the Holy Spirit upon us that gives us access into the realms of spiritual power and authority. That is why God promised that in the last days there will be a tremendous release of His Spirit upon all flesh. The prophet Joel saw into these last days of distinction and prophesied that

> "[28] And afterward,
> I will pour out my Spirit on all people.
> Your sons and daughters will prophesy,
> your old men will dream dreams,
> your young men will see visions.
> [29] Even on my servants, both men and women,
> I will pour out my Spirit in those days" (Joel 2:28-29).

Because of the anointing that these last days saints will walk in, miracles will become commonplace. As some of God's generals who are currently walking in the miraculous have said, healing and deliverance will become like breathing because of the massive outpouring of the Spirit of God. I refuse to settle for anything less than the full manifestation of the power and authority of the cross that comes through the anointing of the Holy Spirit. God is about affirming the words of His servants in a greater measure than He did in the days of the early church.

Do you remember, the Bible says, "Then the disciples went out and preached everywhere, and the Lord worked with them and confirmed his word by the signs that accompanied it" (Mk 16:20) and "So Paul and Barnabas spent considerable time there, speaking boldly for the Lord, who confirmed the message of his grace by enabling them to perform signs and wonders" (Acts 14:3)?

> *Refuse to settle for anything less than the full manifestation of the power and authority of the cross that comes through the anointing of the Holy Spirit. God is about affirming the words of His servants in a greater measure than He did in the days of the early church.*

As we step out in faith to do the Lord's work with a passion to see His kingdom come and nothing less, we will position ourselves for the outpouring promised us and see divine confirmations of our mandate. Until now, the miraculous has been spectacular, but in these days of distinction when the Lord is about to separate His own from those who are not His, when He is about to separate the wheat from the chaff, miracles, signs and wonders will become ordinary. Men who will not walk in power and authority that come from the anointing of the Spirit of the living God will have a hard time proving their credibility.

The Lord Jesus told those who did not believe that He was sent from God, "I did tell you, but you do not believe. The works I do in my Father's name testify about me" (Jn 10:25). The works that God will do through you are what will testify about you in these last days of distinction. We must position ourselves in such a way that we can boldly say to the skeptics, "Do not believe me unless I do the works of my Father. But if I do them, even though you do not believe me, believe the works that you may know and understand that the Father is in me, and I in the Father" (Jn 10:37-38).

These days, men and women are seeking for confirmation that God is using His servants. Those who do not step into the realm of power and authority will have a hard time doing the work of the gospel. Though it costs you everything you own, pursue a relationship with the Spirit of God, and out of that relationship will flow power and authority, evidenced by miracles, signs and wonders.

As you read the Acts of the Apostles, you realize that Paul walked in this dimension of power, and so did the other Apostles and disciples of the Lord like Stephen, Philip the Evangelist, Barnabas and the others. However, it seems as though Paul discovered that there was something more than just the second dimension of power.

It is so sad to see that while Paul was dissatisfied even with the second dimension of power; most of us are satisfied operating in the first dimension of power or in the beginning stages of the second dimension. We need to experience the fullness of the second dimension of power to witness and crave for something more, the demonstration of the resurrection power. This leads us to our next dimension.

The third dimension of power

This is the dimension the Bible calls the incomparably great power of God or the power of His resurrection. It is a higher dimension of the Holy Spirit's power than just the power to testify. It is a foretaste of the powers of the world to come. Paul said, "[10] I want to know Christ—yes, to know the power of his resurrection and participation in his sufferings, becoming like him in his death, [11] and so, somehow, attaining to the resurrection from the dead" (Php 3:10 – 11).

It is evident that Paul walked in spiritual power, the power of the Holy Spirit to bear testimony of the death and resurrection of Jesus through the working of signs, miracles, and wonders. However he craved for something deeper, something he had not yet experienced. This is what he decided to call the power of His resurrection.

Again it was not something for a privileged few; it is for all believers, those who will pay the price to walk in it. However, we must prove faithful in the second dimension of the power to be witnesses of Jesus. We must experience the full dimension of the power to witness with evidence of signs, wonders, and miracles of all sorts in order to be positioned for the next dimension of power. To show that dimension three is not for a chosen few, Paul prayed for the whole church in Ephesus, that they all may come to experience this incomparably great power:

> I pray that the eyes of your heart may be enlightened in order that you may know the hope to which he has called you, the riches of his glorious inheritance in his holy people, and his incomparably great power for us who believe. That power is the same as the mighty strength he exerted when he raised Christ from the dead and seated him at his right hand in the heavenly realms, far above all rule and authority, power and dominion, and every name that is invoked, not only in the present age but also in the one to come. And God placed all things under his feet and appointed him to be head over everything for the church, which is

his body, the fullness of him who fills everything in every way" (Eph 1:18-23).

It is in this dimension that one tastes of the power of the world to come or the powers of the coming age, which Paul spoke about in Hebrews. I believe, in these days of distinction many are going to experience this realm of power of the age to come. In other words power beyond what any created entity has experienced, whether they be mortals or rulers, powers, authorities, and dominions in the invisible realm.

How to position yourself for power and authority

To walk in the power and authority that God has deposited in you as a result of the new birth and the baptism of the Holy Spirit, you will have to release the power from within you through several channels. The more open the channels the greater the power that will flow through you. Let me touch on some of the key channels with you.

I believe, in these days of distinction many are going to experience this realm of power of the age to come. In other words power beyond what any created entity has experienced, whether they be mortals or rulers, powers, authorities, and dominions in the invisible realm.

Brokenness

This is one of the greatest channels for the release of God's power in your life. If you look at history, the servants of God who have wielded the most power in God have been those who have also experienced the most brokenness. God allows His servants to go through experiences that will break open the cap that locks His power in their lives so that it can flow from within them to touch and transform the lives of others. This channel is in the hands of God as He chooses the experiences we go through that make us broken.

Unbroken vessels can only wield a limited amount of power compared to what they would have wielded were they broken. For that reason do not run away from situations and circumstances that will break your pride, self-will, and any such thing that needs to be broken so that you can become an effective instrument in the hands of the Master Potter to form the vessel of His choice. God only uses broken vessels which He has remolded into His likeness.

Prayer

Prayer is another channel for the release of the divine power that is stored up in you as a result of the new birth and the baptism of the Holy Spirit. No one who neglects the avenue of prayer can wield any significant spiritual power. Every one of God's servant who is walking in spiritual power will credit this power to his/her life of prayer. It is sad that sometimes we have thought that we can do without prayer. Because this is not a book on prayer, I will not delve into the how and why of prayer here. Suffice it to say that if you want to walk in extraordinary power, you must make extraordinary prayers. The Spirit only moves as men pray.

Waiting

To wait on the Lord is to spend time with God to listen to what He has to say and give Him the opportunity to renew one in the spirit. It is to keep one's mind and heart focused on the Lord in total quietness and inward worship. Waiting can be incorporated into your prayer time or can be a separate time of just retreating from the humdrum of your schedule to be alone with the Lord. Those who wait on God receive fresh fire, fresh shower, and fresh power from on high.

Fasting

Fasting is another great avenue for the release of spiritual power. When combined with prayer or with waiting on the Lord, it enlarges these channels to at least twice their normal volume of flow. There are several books on the how and why of fasting, procuring one or two will be a great investment.

Word Encounter

Word encounter is more than just casual reading or study of the word. It is the art of meditating on the word and allowing the Holy Spirit to make the written word come alive with respect to your personal need. This is when the word gets hold of the spirit, or should I say when your spirit gets hold of the word. This enliven word becomes like a dynamite that will blow off barriers and put your enemy to flight. There is tremendous power in the word when it is made alive by the Holy Spirit and absorbed by the human spirit. The enliven word becomes the hammer that breaks down barriers; it becomes the fire that consumes the chaff and stubble around you, and the sword that separates the authentic from the fake. Spend quality time with the word and experience boundless power.

Faith

This is what I call the valve of all the channels just mentioned above. No matter how much power can flow through prayer, brokenness, fasting, and word encounter, if the valves are not open through faith, the power will remain locked up in the channels. And you know when power is locked up in the channel through which it flows, pressure builds up and the next thing you know is an accident, if the flow is not stopped at the source. This is why sometimes God has to stop the flow of His power into us until we get to release it through faith. Until you step out in faith to release the power, every other channel will soon be reduced to meaningless routine because the owner of the power will cut it off at the source in order to preserve the vessel.

> *There is tremendous power in the word when it is made alive by the Holy Spirit and absorbed by the human spirit. The enliven word becomes the hammer that breaks down barriers; it becomes the fire that consumes the chaff and stubble around you, and the sword that separates the authentic from the fake.*

CHAPTER 5

VICTORY AND DOMINION

Another area of distinction in these last days will be in exercising victory and dominion. Until now many Christians have led battered, trampled-down lives, beaten down by the circumstances that seem to endlessly stand in opposition to their chosen course. Others are living a life of defeat to sin and all shades of compromise with the world and the things of the world. The majority in the church have never entered their blood bought victory and dominion over the enemy and his cohort.

Because we have allowed the ways of the world to creep into our lives and churches we have become powerless and helpless in the face of the end-time demonic onslaught. Because we have neglected carrying His presence and trusted in our own strength and schemes, the victory that comes from His abiding presence has eluded us one way or the other.

Defeat is sometimes a tool in the hands of the Master Potter to mold us into His likeness. However, a defeated way of life, as is evident with many, should not be the portion of any who calls on His holy Name. We are destined and reborn for victory, triumph and dominion. Because I treated this topic in detail in my book "Living the Triumphant Life", I will not discuss it broadly here, however I will touch on some vital aspects of victory, dominion and triumph we are going to witness in these last days of distinction. Those who rightly position themselves are in to experience unprecedented victory and dominion.

Your inheritance in Christ
"But thanks be to God, Who gives us the victory [making us conquerors] through our Lord Jesus Christ" (1Co 15:57, AMP).

"Yet amid all these things we are more than conquerors and gain a surpassing victory through Him Who loved us" (Ro 8:37, AMP).

In these days of distinction, God is making us to walk in continuous victory and triumph over all the forces that are assailing us. I like that Paul puts the verse in the present continuous, that is, God is constantly giving us the victory. Victory is not a one-time thing, nor is it something of the past, but it is current and functional in the lives of those who live in Christ consciousness.

Remember, the victory is through Jesus Christ our Lord. The closer we walk with Him the greater the victory we experience. As we distinguish ourselves as carriers of His presence, we automatically distinguish ourselves in terms of victory and triumph. The second verse cited above says we gain a surpassing victory. The word surpassing means outstanding, superior, exceptional victory. So the kind of victory we are going to walk in in these last days is uncommon. We are

> *Because we have allowed the ways of the world to creep into our lives and churches we have become powerless and helpless in the face of the end-time demonic onslaught*

positioning ourselves for victory that is more than what conquerors experience. Yet the victory is "through Him who loved us". It is our Christ consciousness, our awareness of His love for us and His victory over the forces of evil, which positions us to walk in outstanding dominion.

How to align yourself for victory
1. Live with Christ consciousness:

When you fill your mind and heart with thoughts of Christ's victory over the enemy and his cohorts, you are taking the first step towards living in uncommon dominion. And when you stay conscious of the fact that He has equipped and positioned you for victory and triumph over the enemy you will live an invincible life. You have been destined to reign in life in Christ Jesus. This leads us to our next point.

2. Live grace – conscious:

"For if, by the trespass of the one man, death reigned through that one man, how much more will those who receive God's abundant provision of grace and of the gift of righteousness reign in life through the one man, Jesus Christ!" (Ro 5:17).

God has made available His infinite grace as an ever present resource to position His children for victory. His grace is available to enable even the feeblest among His people live a victorious overcoming life. There are two conditions in the verse cited above that position us for victory: the first is that we are to have received God's abundant provision of grace. The second is that we are to have received God's abundant provision of the gift of righteousness.

These two conditions are core requisites for anyone who claims to be born again. Therefore every child of God should reign in life. But the truth is that most of our experiences are contrary to this, because we try to reign by human effort and by our own righteousness instead of the gift of righteousness. This leads to guilt and condemnation and therefore defeat and death.

As wickedness is increasing in the world in these days so is the grace of God made increasingly abundant to enable His people walk in victory above the traps of sin, defeat, and death.

3. Be a carrier of the divine presence

"No one will be able to stand against you all the days of your life. As I was with Moses, so I will be with you; I will never leave you nor forsake you" (Jos 1:5). The presence of Jehovah with Joshua ensured that none of his enemies could stand up against him, let alone defeat him. If we are not experiencing the same victory, we must carry the presence of God as Moses did. We are to experience the glory in greater measure than Moses because we are living in the glory dispensation, given that we have been glorified with Christ. We must be ready to abide in His presence until His glory flows through us and terrorizes whatever does not align with His divine nature.

4. The anointing of the Lord:

"Now this I know: The Lord gives victory to his anointed. He answers him from his heavenly sanctuary with the victorious power of his right hand. Some trust in chariots and some in horses, but we trust in the name of the Lord our God. They are brought to their knees and fall, but we rise up and stand firm" (Ps 20:6-8).

You are destined for victory when God's anointing is upon your life. The anointing breaks the yoke of oppression and limitation. The Lord is bound to ensure victory when He sees the anointing of the Spirit in operation upon a life. It will break every yoke of limitation and set a standard against the onslaught of the enemy in your life. The anointing will lead you to avoid the traps of defeat and failure the enemy has set on your path. This leads us to the next point.

5. Total dependence on, and absolute trust in the Lord:

"Give us aid against the enemy, for human help is worthless. ^{13} With God we will gain the victory, and he will trample down our enemies" (Ps 108: 12-13).

"You are my King and my God,
who decrees victories for Jacob.
^{5} Through you we push back our enemies;
through your name we trample our foes.
^{6} I put no trust in my bow,
my sword does not bring me victory;
^{7} but you give us victory over our enemies,
you put our adversaries to shame.

⁸ In God we make our boast all day long,
and we will praise your name forever" (Ps 44:4-8).

You must take the Name of Jesus with you wherever you go and whatever you do in order to walk in absolute victory. God has decreed victory for you, but you've got to enforce the decree through the power of the Name of the Almighty, King of kings and Lord of lords. Come to the point where you place your trust in nothing but the Name of the Lord, then you will watch your adversaries be put to shame and clothed with disgrace. God wants to make you rise up and stand firm where others are being brought to their knees; this will make you distinct from those who do not bear that Name.

6. Stay humble:

"For the Lord takes delight in his people; he crowns the humble with victory" (Ps 149:4).

There is a place of victorious living where an individual wears victory like a crown. The pathway to this place is humility. Those who humble themselves before the Lord are made victorious in every aspect of their lives because they wear victory as a crown. One important aspect of humility is to do all in the Name of the Lord and for the glory of God. At all cost stay humble and enjoy endless victory.

> *Defeat is sometimes a tool in the hands of the Master Potter to mold us into His likeness. However, a defeated way of life, as is evident with many, should not be the portion of any who calls on His holy Name.*

CHAPTER 6
DIVINE FAVOR

Favor from above is one important element that produces distinction in the lives of people. Favor will distinguish you from the masses and position you to operate entirely from another dimension. If you look at Bible history you will realize that favor in the lives of men and women distinguished them from their contemporaries. Favor, when bestowed on a man or woman, boy or girl will make his or her destiny, and the lack of it may mar his or her destiny. Throughout scripture, you find individuals whose situations were changed for the better because they found favor with God and man.

If John the Baptist was right, and I believe he was, then you can only find favor with men if favor has been bestowed on you from Heaven's courts. For He said, "a man can receive only what is given him from Heaven" (Jn 3: 27).

To succeed in life, you need both favor with God and favor before man. Of the boy Samuel, it is said, "And the boy Samuel continued to grow in stature and in favor with the Lord and with men" (1 Sam 2: 26). Any doubt Samuel had such a successful ministry in the three fold capacity of priest, prophet and Judge in Israel?

What about the only Begotten, Sovereign and Eternal Son of God? It is written, "And Jesus grew in wisdom and stature, and in favor with God and men" (Luke 2: 52). If God's Son needed favor before God and man, then you and I need it more, even more than we know or think. Why was Mary chosen to be the mother of the Savior of Mankind? Because she found favor with the God of creation! (see Luke 1: 30).

What took Esther to the throne of the Persian Empire? Nothing but favor!

"Now the king was attracted to Esther more than to any of the other women, and she won his favor and approval more than any of the other virgins. So he set a royal crown on her head and made her queen instead of Vashti" (Esther 2: 17).

Do you realize it was because of favor that Abraham became a host of divinity? He said to the angels (amongst whom was the Angel of the Lord Himself), "My Lord, if now I have found favor in Your sight, please do not pass Your servant by" (Ge 18:3, NASB). This means the Lord was going to pass by Abraham but because Abraham found favor before the Lord, God stopped in His tracks to have dinner with a man. Is that not wonderful? Favor caused a man to dine with

> *Favor will distinguish you from the masses and position you to operate entirely from another dimension... To succeed in life, you need both favor with God and favor before man.*

Jehovah. That kind of visitation was not common, but favor so distinguished Abraham from his contemporaries that divinity visited with him.

Do you remember David? It is written that he enjoyed God's favor (see Acts 7:46). That is why David still stands out in the history of mankind as a king like no other.

How to obtain favor
1. Develop passion:

David enjoyed God's favor because he was a man after God's heart. When you set your heart ablaze in pursuit of the divine you position yourself to attract divine favor. Divinity responds to passionate pursuits from hearts that are desperate to see His kingdom come, and His will established in the hearts of humankind.

2. Obedience.

Obedience is an open door to favor with man. If you want to find favor you've got to be obedient. Esther's favor before Hegai was certainly due to her obedient attitude from childhood as suggested in verse twenty of chapter two:

Now, the Bible says, "And this is how she would go to the king: Anything she wanted was given her to take with her from the harem to the king's palace" (Esther 2: 13).

Anyone could ask for whatever she wanted to take into the king's presence in order to win the king's approval. There was freedom of choice according to one's taste. Now, listen to this,

"When the turn came for Esther (the girl Mordecai had adopted, the daughter of his uncle Abihail) to go to the king, she asked for nothing other than what Hegai, the king's eunuch who was in charge of the harem, suggested. And Esther won the favor of everyone who saw her" (Esther 2: 15).

Her obedience to Modecai caused her to find favor with Hegai, and her obedience to Hegai, caused her to find favor with everyone who saw her and subsequently favor with the king. Obedience courts favor more than you can ever imagine (see Leviticus 26).

3. Holiness:

Living in holiness and righteousness opens the way for favor from the King of Righteousness. In a world where unrighteousness seems to be on the rise, living holy will cause you to find favor before the God of holiness.

"But Noah found favor in the eyes of the LORD. This is the account of Noah. Noah was a righteous man, blameless among the people of his time, and he walked with God" (Gen 6: 8 - 9).

Verse 9 gives us the reason why Noah found favor with God.

- He was righteous

- He was blameless

- He walked with God.

Holiness makes way for the favor of God's anointing to rest upon an individual. About the Messiah, it is said,

"You have loved righteousness and hated wickedness; therefore God, your God, has set you above your companions by anointing you with the oil of joy" (He1: 9).

Do you need the favor of God's anointing in your ministry, then live holy, set your heart on righteousness! Even the Psalmist knew this and said, "For surely, O LORD, you bless the righteous and surround them with your favor as with a shield" (Ps 5: 12).

4. Love and Faithfulness:

"Let love and faithfulness never leave you; bind them around your neck, write them on the tablet of your heart. Then you will win favor and a good name in the sight of God and man" (Pr 3: 3 - 4).

Another gateway into the land of favor with God and with man is to live in love - love towards God and towards man - and to practice faithfulness in whatever your hand finds to do and more so in your duty and calling as a Christian.

5. Wisdom:

"Whoever finds me finds life and receives favor from the LORD" (Pr 8: 35).

As you seek and find wisdom from the LORD, He bestows on you His favor. Why? Because wisdom will lead you on the path of righteousness and justice! Wisdom will lead you to understand the ways of God and to act with prudence. Go in for wisdom, seek and find wisdom and along with it you will receive God's infinite favor.

6. Knowing the ways of the Lord

"Now therefore, I pray You, if I have found favor in Your sight, let me know Your ways that I may know You, so that I may find favor in Your sight" (Ex 33: 13a, NASB).

This is like a two way chemical reaction, when you find favor in God's sight, He reveals to you His ways that make you to know Him better. When you know God's ways, it causes you to find increasing favor in His sight. Thus you are always growing in favor and in knowledge of God.

What favor does

(1) Favor will spare you from wrath

"But Noah found favor in the eyes of the LORD"(Gen 6: 8).

At the brink of God's judgment upon renegade humanity, Noah's favor with God caused him and his family to be spared and preserved. That which money or education cannot buy, favor will bring.

(2) Favor will cause you to behold God's glory

(See Ex 33: 12 - 23).

Because Moses found favor with God, God was "forced" to reveal His glory to Moses even in the midst of His anger against the children of Israel.

(3) Favor will cause you to be fruitful

"I will look on you with favor and make you fruitful and increase your numbers, and I will keep my covenant with you" (Lev 26: 9).

God's favor upon you will make you fruitful in all that you do. Favor brings in a supernatural multiplying factor to the harvest of whatever you lay your hands on. The secret to financial fruitfulness, spiritual fruitfulness, fruitfulness of the womb etc. is to win the Lord's favor.

(4) Favor will cause your offering to be accepted

"But Abel brought fat portions from some of the firstborn of his flock. The LORD looked with favor on Abel and his offering" (Gen 4: 4).

"Gideon replied, "If now I have found favor in your eyes, give me a sign that it is really you talking to me" (Judges 6: 17).

Our God is a great king, who chooses what to accept from whoever is making the offering. Favor with God will cause Him to accept your offering. Actually it is a privilege to give to Him and it is an honor when He accepts your offerings.

(5) Favor brings about Victory.

"It was not by their sword that they won the land, nor did their arm bring them victory; it was your right hand, your arm, and the light of your face, for you loved them" (Ps 44: 3).

What does "the light of your face" signify but God's favor? In this generation where people depend on their strength and weapons, go beyond that to seeking the Lord's favor. That is what brings victory. Do you remember the Aaronic blessing?

"The LORD bless you and keep you; the LORD make his face shine upon you and be gracious to you; the LORD turn his face toward you and give you peace." (Num 6: 24 - 26)

It is nothing but God's favor; making His face to shine upon you and turning His face towards you speak of nothing but His favor.

(6) Favor brings His peace.

"Glory to God in the highest, and on earth peace to men on whom his favor rests"(Luke 2: 14).

The peace of God is on those who have found favor with Him. The Bible says, God "gives sleep to those he loves". The King James Version translates sleep as rest, and what is there in rest but peace, peace with yourself, with man and above all with God.

> *God's favor upon you will make you fruitful in all that you do. Favor brings in a supernatural multiplying factor to the harvest of whatever you lay your hands on. The secret to financial fruitfulness, spiritual fruitfulness, fruitfulness of the womb etc. is to win the Lord's favor.*

CHAPTER 7
THE LIGHT AND GLORY OF GOD

As you fly over cities or towns or villages at night, what distinguishes them from thousands of feet above sea level is the intensity of light within those areas of human habitation. Darkness has the capacity to reveal the intensity of light that objects give off. It is for the same reason that you are able to distinguish the stars from hundreds of light years away. In these last days of distinction, as thick darkness covers the earth so will a greater glory rise upon God's people. The Lord says:

> "Arise, shine, for your light has come,
> and the glory of the Lord rises upon you.
> ² See, darkness covers the earth
> and thick darkness is over the peoples,
> but the Lord rises upon you
> and his glory appears over you.

> ³ Nations will come to your light,
> and kings to the brightness of your dawn" (Is 60:1-3).

In these days the difference will be made clearer than ever before. You will either be shinning with utmost brightness or be engulfed in the thickest darkest. Do you remember when there was darkness all over Egypt, but the children of Israel had light? This scene was prophetic of what we are entering into these last days. Let's take a look at the passage:

> "²¹Then the Lord said to Moses, "Stretch out your hand toward the sky so that darkness spreads over Egypt—darkness that can be felt." ²² So Moses stretched out his hand toward the sky, and total darkness covered all Egypt for three days. ²³ No one could see anyone else or move about for three days. Yet all the Israelites had light in the places where they lived" (Ex 10:21-23).

There will be no middle ground in these last days just as there was no middle ground in those days in Egypt. The darkness will be so thick that it will be felt by those engulfed in it. However, those who have taken their stand in righteousness have nothing to fear, because while there will be palpable darkness over those who do not belong to the Lord, there will be palpable glory over the people of God.

> *Darkness has the capacity to reveal the intensity of light that objects give off. .. In these last days of distinction, as thick darkness covers the earth so will a greater glory rise upon God's people.*

When the world beholds the glory over us and the light emanating from us, they will have no option but to come to us for shelter. The light streaming from around us will attract the nations and kings of the world. Of course, as they come they bring along all they have accumulated. If you continue to read the other verses of Isaiah 60, you see that the wealth of the nations will be brought to us the chosen of the Lord, because of the glory that is already rising on the people of God.

Glory that exalts

The Psalmist said "But you, Lord, are a shield around me, my glory, the One who lifts my head high" (Ps 3:3). When you connect to the glory then you are bound for uplifting by God. The purpose of the glory is to lift up your head above your contemporaries, and more so above your enemies. As the glory of God rises upon you in these days of distinction, it will set you above those who will otherwise be above you.

Nothing uplifts and promotes, beyond imagination, like when you get connected to the glory. In these days of distinction I see you rising higher than you ever expected because the Lord will lift up your head. I see your head being raised higher than those of your competitors because you are being surrounded by the glory.

The Canopy of Glory

"⁵Then the Lord will create over all of Mount Zion and over those who assemble there a cloud of smoke by day and a glow of flaming fire by night; over everything the glory will be a canopy. ⁶It will be a shelter and shade from the heat of the day, and a refuge and hiding place from the storm and rain" (Is 4:5-6).

As the glory rises upon the church of Christ in these last days, it will form a canopy. You know a canopy is used to provide shade and shelter from the elements; it is for covering. The amount of glory that rises upon you these last days will determine the strength, thickness, and resistance of the canopy that will be over you.

The Bible passage above says, "over everything the glory will be a canopy". Over your home the glory will be a canopy; over your job the glory will be a canopy, over your body, marriage, ministry, finances,

> *While there will be palpable darkness over those who do not belong to the Lord, there will be palpable glory over the people of God... Over your home the glory will be a canopy; over your job the glory will be a canopy, over your body, marriage, ministry, finances, relationships and any other thing that concerns you, the glory is going to be a canopy.*

relationships and any other thing that concerns you, the glory is going to be a canopy.

My friend this is crucial, your safety and security depends on the glory you will carry in these days of thick and palpable darkness over the earth. No aspect of your life should be left out of the glory. The glory will be your shade and shelter from the rain, sun, and storms of life. It will be your shield from the evil flaming darts of the enemy.

This is a place of absolute safety and security. This is no longer an option for a selected few; it is the means of survival and thriving for all who are on Mount Zion. You must press on until you breakthrough the veil into the realm of glory. I feel motivated like never before to dwell in this place of safety.

We saw earlier that the nations and kings will come to our light and to the brightness of our dawn. In other words when they behold the risen glory upon us, the only solution from the thick darkness is to seek shelter in the light and the glory. As we allow the glory to envelop us then what the prophet Isaiah proclaimed thousands of years ago will become reality: "Each one will be like a shelter from the wind and a refuge from the storm, like streams of water in the desert and the shadow of a great rock in a thirsty land" (Is 32:2).

The nations will come to us for shelter from the winds and storms that will ravage the world. They will come to drink that water of life that will be bubbling from within us. This promise is why you cannot afford to settle for anything less than being enveloped by the glory of the great God.

How to activate the glory

When the children of Israel, under the leadership of Moses, were in the wilderness, God gave Moses instructions to pass on to Aaron and the children of Israel so that His glory may appear to them:

"6 Then Moses said, "This is what the Lord has commanded you to do, so that the glory of the Lord may appear to you" (Lev 9:6).

In other words there are procedures to follow in order to be overshadowed and enveloped by the glory of the great God. I sense the Lord is saying the same thing to us today, to get ready to be enveloped by the glory of God. Let us see the instructions that Moses gave to Aaron and the Israelites.

> On the eighth day Moses summoned Aaron and his sons and the elders of Israel. ² He said to Aaron, "Take a bull calf for your sin offering and a ram for your burnt offering, both without defect, and present them before the Lord. ³ Then say to the Israelites: 'Take a male goat for a sin

offering, a calf and a lamb—both a year old and without defect—for a burnt offering, [4] and an ox and a ram for a fellowship offering to sacrifice before the Lord, together with a grain offering mixed with olive oil. For today the Lord will appear to you'" (Lev 9:1-4).

The following vital points emerge from the above instructions:

1. They were to offer sin offerings
2. They were to offer burnt offerings
3. They were to offer fellowship offerings
4. They were to offer grain offerings

The Sin Offering

The sin offering was for the purpose of atonement. This part has already been fulfilled by God offering His Son as sacrifice for sin on our behalf. So God has taken the first step for the release of His glory. However we have to accept this sacrifice and constantly be connected to it through confession and repentance. The good thing is that God went further to clothe us with His own righteousness through the gift of Jesus. Therefore we have fulfilled the first condition for the release of the glory. All we have to do is to confess and completely forsake any sin in our lives.

The Burnt Offering

The burnt offering was meant to raise a permanent altar for the Israelite. It was a kind of continuous prayer offered to the Lord on behalf of the Israelites. The fire on the altar of burnt offering was supposed to be a continuous fire before the Lord. That is why Paul said we should pray without ceasing. Again the Lord has made this easier to be fulfilled in us. When we are filled with the Holy Spirit we can be in the spirit of prayer by always praying in tongues. We pray in tongues silently or audible depending on where we are and in this way the fire on the altar of our hearts will be kept continually burning before the Lord God of hosts. The Holy Spirit is your prayer partner to help you keep the fire as you let Him pray through you.

The Fellowship offering

The fellowship offering could be made for three reasons: as an expression of thankfulness to the Lord, as a fulfillment of a vow made to God, or as a freewill offering (see lev 7: 11-21). Hence there are three ways to maintain fellowship with the Lord: by offering thanks to the Lord, by fulfilling vows, commitments, and pledges to God; and by giving freewill offerings to God. So to be enveloped by the glory in these days of distinction, one has to live a life of gratitude to the Lord. Thankfulness establishes fellowship with the Godhead and opens a channel for the release of his glory.

Those who are to experience the glory must be those who make commitments to God and fulfill them. We live in an age where people make commitments during emotional highs and thereafter abandon them. Such tendencies block you from experiencing and being enveloped by the glory. You must be a man or woman of your word. Say only what you mean, and mean everything you say. This will open the avenue for fellowship with God and create a channel for the flow of His glory into your life.

Last, but not the least factor is that those who must experience the glory are those who are ready to offer freewill offerings to the Lord. Such people give to God not out of compulsion or mere obligation but because they are head-over-heels for God. You remember Solomon? He gave freely to God beyond the normal requirement or mere obligation and activated a release of the glory.

The Grain Offering

The grain offering signified worship and praise to Jehovah. The grain offering that the priests offered on their own behalf had to be burned completely to the Lord. They were to share no part of that offering brought to the Lord on their own behalf although they were permitted to eat a portion of the offering that was made by the general population. This means that in the New Testament dispensation where we all have become priests, our grain offering should be offered entirely to God. We cannot partake of it.

As priests of the New Covenant, we have been called to share in everything God receives except the worship and praise that is due Him. If we must experience the glory we must make sure we give God all the glory and praise all the time. It is His portion that must be offered regularly by all those who have been made priests of the New Covenant. So in these days of distinction those who are to experience the glory are those who will give themselves for worship to the great God, Three in One.

Now when all the instructions of the Lord had been followed something more happened before the glory manifested. The Bible says,

> Then Aaron lifted his hands toward the people and blessed them. And having sacrificed the sin offering, the burnt offering and the fellowship offering, he stepped down. [23] Moses and Aaron then went into the tent of meeting. When they came out, they blessed the people; and the glory of the Lord appeared to all the people. [24] Fire came out from the presence of the Lord and consumed the burnt offering and the fat portions on the altar. And when all the people saw it, they shouted for joy and fell facedown (Lev 9:22-24).

These verses reveal two additional conditions before the glory showed up:

5. Moses and Aaron blessed the people

Those who are committed to bless the people of God are enveloped by His glory and given the mandate to release it to others. They do not seek to profit from serving God's people or exercise oppressive power over them, but are committed in earnest to see God's people walk in abundance of blessing. They are quick to bless than to curse, quick to appreciate than to criticize, quick to encourage than to castigate and through them God will release the glory. He will envelop them with His glory.

6. Aaron stepped down

There are many people who fulfill the first five points already mentioned; what keeps them from experiencing the glory is that they have remained up when they need to step down. Sometimes we have to "step down", not in the sense of resignation, but to allow God to do His thing. We often stand in God's way of releasing His glory because we step up with our ideas, past experiences, and desire to share His glory. If we like Aaron step down in earnest and give God "space" to do His thing, we will be surprised by the results.

Be ready to step back and let God take the lead, step down and let His glory show up. When Aaron stepped down, God showed up in His glory; the people shouted for joy and fell down in worship. I have heard people say "God's glory is here", but the greater part of the people present are seated or distracted. Man, when God's glory shows up everyone is forced to fall prostrate or look for a place to hide.

Vertical and Horizontal Constraints

Now, these were God's instruction to Moses for His glory to manifest amongst the congregation. If you took note five out of the six points had to do with our relationship with God, and one had to do with our relationship with man. The next passage I want to share with you will bring more points on how our relationship with man will release a manifestation of the glory in our lives. Because the passage is somehow long, I will encourage you to read it carefully on your own. I will cite only the verses that we need here, but reading the entire passage will give you a fuller picture. Take some time and read the entire chapter of Isaiah 58.

> *Be ready to step back and let God take the lead, step down and let His glory show up. When Aaron stepped down, God showed up in His glory; the people shouted for joy and fell down in worship.*

"Is not this the kind of fasting I have chosen:
to loose the chains of injustice
and untie the cords of the yoke,
to set the oppressed free
and break every yoke?

⁷ Is it not to share your food with the hungry
and to provide the poor wanderer with shelter—
when you see the naked, to clothe them,
and not to turn away from your own flesh and blood?
⁸ ***Then your light will break forth like the dawn,***
and your healing will quickly appear;
then your righteousness will go before you,
and the glory of the Lord will be your rear guard.
⁹ Then you will call, and the Lord will answer;
you will cry for help, and he will say: Here am I.

"If you do away with the yoke of oppression,
with the pointing finger and malicious talk,
¹⁰ and if you spend yourselves in behalf of the hungry
and satisfy the needs of the oppressed,
***then your light will rise in the darkness,
and your night will become like the noonday.***

(Is 58: 6-10, emphases mine throughout)

Remember, in this chapter we have been talking about the light and the glory of God, and the role they play to make us distinct in these last days. Here the Lord gives several "if...then..." statements that deal with the release of the glory and the brilliance of our light. Interestingly, every single one of these conditions for the release of the glory and the brightness of our light has to do with our relationship with fellow man. And this is why many of us who have qualified through our relationship with God as we saw earlier have failed to behold His glory. Let us continue with the conditions for activating the glory we started in our passage from Leviticus.

7. Be freedom and justice minded

Verses 6 and 9b of our passage above, from Isaiah, talk about the need to work for justice for the oppressed and to lose the chains of bondage of those who are bound. If you must experience the glory, you must have a mind to see people set free from every manner of bondage that is operating in their lives. Have a passion to see people delivered from the oppressive power of the evil one, and his yokes broken off the neck of the sons and daughters of men.

When God sees such a passion for freedom and justice, He will release His glory because the glory will make it easier for you to bring freedom and justice to those suffering from satanic oppression and bondage in any form. You cannot be indifferent towards the suffering of men and position yourself for the glory. If

God should release His glory to one who is indifferent then such a one will only use it for self-advertisement and vain personal display; God is not interested in any of that.

8. Be compassionate and generous

Verses 7 and 10a talk of the need for compassion and generosity towards the weak and needy all around us. Share your food with the hungry, clothe the naked, and provide shelter for the homeless. Let God's heart of compassion beat within you as you meet the needs that are in your power and ability to meet. Instead of passing judgment, show mercy and flow in compassion.

When these happen you open the way for a manifestation of the glory in your life. The Lord says your light will break forth like the dawn and God's glory will be your rear guard. In other words, the light that will shine from you will be breaking forth as you move forward while the glory is taking care of your back. What a blessed and glorious way to live; light before you and the glory behind you!

And finally, the Lord says your night will become like noonday. When your night becomes like noon day it means your life will not have any night. You know the night is the time when evil works. Prostitutes go out mostly at night. Thieves go out mostly at night, witches and wizards go out mostly at night, the Bible even talks of the terror that flies by night. So when there is no more night in your life, you have entered another dimension of glory. You have a foretaste of the life of heaven here on earth. That is what the light and the glory can do.

> *When God sees such a passion for freedom and justice, He will release His glory because the glory will make it easier for you to bring freedom and justice to those suffering from satanic oppression and bondage in any form. You cannot be indifferent towards the suffering of men and position yourself for the glory.*

CHAPTER 8

HOLINESS

If you remember, we had said at the beginning of this study that God is committed to make a distinction between the righteous and the wicked. These days, it seems as if the lines between holiness and wickedness have been blurred as the sins of the world are fast creeping into the church and certain practices that were unacceptable just a few years ago are now becoming a common practice even for those who call on His holy Name.

I am not referring to those sins as homosexuality and abortion which we all know are hard core wickedness and perversion. What I am referring to are sins like fornication and adultery, greed, falsehood, and hypocrisy which many seem to have settled in as a way of life. Some people when they come to Christ are never taught to separate from, and abandon their old lifestyles. They are made to believe that salvation consists of joining a congregation of God's people. God is again drawing the line between His church and the world, and those who call on His Name should depart from everything that has the appearance of evil.

The Lord told the Israelites, "I am the Lord, who brought you up out of Egypt to be your God; therefore be holy, because I am holy" (Lev 11:45). God's standard of holiness for those He saves out of the world is nothing less than the holiness that He embodies. He says "be holy as I am holy", not as your leader is holy, not as your neighbor is holy, not as your brethren are holy, but be holy as the Lord Himself is holy. I hear someone saying but that is the Old Testament. My response to you is that Peter wrote, "[14] As obedient children, do not conform to the evil desires you had when you lived in ignorance. [15] But just as he who called you is holy, so be holy in all you do; [16] for it is written: "Be holy, because I am holy" (1Pe 1:14-16).

The Lord Jesus Himself said, "Be perfect, therefore, as your heavenly Father is perfect" (Mt 5:48). Both Peter and the Lord Jesus use God's holiness as the standard and reference for the holiness the saints have to walk in. This means God's standards have not changed; if anything the standards have grown stricter because of the provision of grace that the Old Testament saints did not have.

Stricter Standards

"You are to be holy to me because I, the Lord, am holy, and I have set you apart from the nations to be my own" (Lev 20:26).

The distinguishing mark the Lord gave the Israelites as His chosen people was that they were to be holy and set apart for Him. Today, it is not

> *God is again drawing the line between His church and the world, and those who call on His Name should depart from everything that has the appearance of evil.*

different; what distinguishes a child of God from the world he/she has been taken out from is that such a person walks in holiness. With a tone of severity, Paul echoes the same demand for the church when he wrote, "But among you there must not be even a hint of sexual immorality, or of any kind of impurity, or of greed, because these are improper for God's holy people" (Eph 5:3).

So as the church of God, we are held to greater and higher standards because of the provision of grace we have received. Grace is divine power made available to us to be able to live the life God has ordained for us through the death of His Son on the cross of Calvary.

Divine enabling
"…to rescue us from the hand of our enemies, and to enable us to serve him without fear in holiness and righteousness before him all our days" (Lk 1:74-75).

Zechariah gave this prophecy about the salvation that God was bringing through the Messiah, for whom his son John had come to prepare the way. The purpose of this salvation was to rescue them from the hands of their enemies and to **enable** them to serve Him without fear in holiness and righteousness.

So, fearless service in holiness and righteousness comes through divine enabling, and not through human effort. All we have to do is accept God's provision for holiness which is Christ Jesus "who has become for us wisdom from God—that is, our righteousness, holiness and redemption" (1Co 1:30). Thus God has fulfilled the requirement for holiness in the person of Jesus Christ. Our sole responsibility is to conform to the life He lives through us.

The Highway of Holiness
"[8]And a highway will be there;
it will be called the Way of Holiness;

> it will be for those who walk on that Way.
> The unclean will not journey on it;
> wicked fools will not go about on it.
> ⁹ No lion will be there,
> nor any ravenous beast;
> they will not be found there.
> But only the redeemed will walk there,
> ¹⁰ and those the Lord has rescued will return.
> They will enter Zion with singing;
> everlasting joy will crown their heads.
> Gladness and joy will overtake them,
> and sorrow and sighing will flee away" (Is 35:8-10).

There is a highway in life that leads to excellence and glory called the Way of Holiness. On this highway only those who live holy are given a pass to ride. Here is where distinction is enforced by God Himself. Any form of uncleanness in your life will disqualify you from riding on this highway. It is a highway of divine encounters and revelation of the King of righteousness. It leads to the land of redemption where the saints enter the fullness of their inheritance in Christ Jesus.

This highway leads to the land of abundant joy and gladness, peace and security. On this highway there are no ferocious beasts. In other words on the highway of holiness there is no fear of harm, because the enemy is not allowed there. He has no access to this highway. It is reserved for those who have been redeemed and are walking in holiness. Won't you choose to live in holiness so that you have access to this road your enemy cannot tread?

> *There is a highway in life that leads to excellence and glory called the Way of Holiness. On this highway only those who live holy are given a pass to ride. Here is where distinction is enforced by God Himself.*

CHAPTER 9

WEALTH AND RICHES

One conspicuous area in life that distinguishes people is the wealth and riches they possess. The truth is that God is not indifferent to us distinguishing ourselves in this area of wealth too. As much as God wants us to prosper spiritually, so does He want us to prosper financially. The Bible says, "Beloved, I wish above all things that thou mayest prosper and be in health, even as thy soul prospereth" (3Jn 2, KJV).

The Lord wishes for us to prosper in our bodies, our souls, and our finances. This is Bible truth; anything else is from the pit of hell. Prosperity is not a sin nor is it apostasy as some misguided believers have made themselves to believe. In these days of distinction the Lord is going to parade His children in abundance of blessings that will make them stand out from those who do not know the Lord.

Wealth without Worries

The people of the world toil, defraud others, or make pacts with the devil in order to become rich and wealthy. Now the difference with the wealth and riches that are coming to the church is that, it is the blessing of the Lord that will make us rich. Here is what the Bible has to say about it: "The blessing of the Lord brings wealth, without painful toil for it" (Pr 10:22).

> The truth is that God is not indifferent to us distinguishing ourselves in this area of wealth too. As much as God wants us to prosper spiritually, so does He want us to prosper financially.

So, it is not the painful toil that takes you away from the place of devotion and intimacy with God, takes you away from your family, and makes you lose all vitality, but it is the supernatural hand of God upon everything you do that will bring you wealth and riches. As you obey the voice of the Holy Spirit, He will lead you to make investments and establish businesses that will lead to extraordinary wealth and riches. He is able to give you revelations that will lead to witty inventions top companies will scramble for.

The Wealth of the Nations

> "Then you will look and be radiant,
> your heart will throb and swell with joy;
> the wealth on the seas will be brought to you,
> to you the riches of the nations will come.
> ⁶ Herds of camels will cover your land,
> young camels of Midian and Ephah.
> And all from Sheba will come,
> bearing gold and incense
> and proclaiming the praise of the Lord.
> ⁷ All Kedar's flocks will be gathered to you,
> the rams of Nebaioth will serve you;
> they will be accepted as offerings on my altar,
> and I will adorn my glorious temple" (Is 60:5-7).

In these last days God is going to orchestrate an exodus of wealth from the nations into the Kingdom of the saints. As the glory of the Lord rises upon His church and the nations come to her light, they will bring along with them all they own, because the church will be the only place of safety. I want you to realize that the Lord is promising both wealth and riches. You see here maritime wealth, agricultural wealth, and mineral wealth. We are entering the season of unprecedented wealth transfer.

As if the wealth transfer is not enough, the Lord says we will also be distinct in the quality of the riches we receive. Where others are being rewarded with bronze, the Lord will ensure that we get gold. Where others are receiving iron, the Lord ensures that we get silver, when they receive wood, we get bronze, and when they receive stones we get iron.

God is saying in every way possible there will be a distinction between the world and the church even in this area of wealth. The Lord says well-being will be your ruler. That is every area of your life will prosper. Get ready and position yourself for distinctive wealth that will come because of the light and the glory that is rising on you.

> *As the glory of the Lord rises upon His church and the nations come to her light, they will bring along with them all they own, because the church will be the only place of safety.*

"You will drink the milk of nations
and be nursed at royal breasts.
Then you will know that I, the Lord, am your Savior,
your Redeemer, the Mighty One of Jacob.
[17] Instead of bronze I will bring you gold,
and silver in place of iron.
Instead of wood I will bring you bronze,
and iron in place of stones.
I will make peace your governor
and well-being your ruler" (Is 60:16-17).

We are entering a season of distinction, not the distinction that comes from competitiveness and covetousness, but one that stems from contentment and commitment to the things of the Kingdom. Position yourself for distinction by staying content with your life and Christ and being committed to the expansion of the Kingdom of God.

> *The Lord says we will also be distinct in the quality of the riches we receive. Where others are being rewarded with bronze, the Lord will ensure that we get gold. Where others are receiving iron, the Lord ensures that we get silver, when they receive wood, we get bronze, and when they receive stones we get iron.*

www.ingramcontent.com/pod-product-compliance
Lightning Source LLC
Chambersburg PA
CBHW020034120526
44588CB00030B/345